POLICE DOGS

BY CYNTHIA ARGENTINE

Apex is distributed by North Star Editions:
sales@northstareditions.com | 888-417-0195

Produced for Apex by Red Line Editorial.

Photographs ©: Shutterstock Images, cover, 1, 4–5, 12–13, 14, 18, 20, 21, 22–23, 24–25, 26, 27; Charles Krupa/AP Images, 6–7, 8; iStockphoto, 10–11, 15, 16–17, 29

Library of Congress Control Number: 2022912277

ISBN
978-1-63738-423-7 (hardcover)
978-1-63738-450-3 (paperback)
978-1-63738-503-6 (ebook pdf)
978-1-63738-477-0 (hosted ebook)

Printed in the United States of America
Mankato, MN
012023

NOTE TO PARENTS AND EDUCATORS

Apex books are designed to build literacy skills in striving readers. Exciting, high-interest content attracts and holds readers' attention. The text is carefully leveled to allow students to achieve success quickly. Additional features, such as bolded glossary words for difficult terms, help build comprehension.

TABLE OF CONTENTS

CHAPTER 1

TO THE RESCUE

A teenage boy is missing. Ruby the police dog goes to work. Nose to the ground, she searches the woods near the boy's house.

Dogs help the police look for people who are lost or in danger.

After several hours, Ruby finds the boy's scent. She follows the smell through the trees. Her **handler** runs after her.

Ruby's handler is a Rhode Island State Trooper. Ruby helps him find people and evidence.

FAST FACT

Police dogs are also called K9s. K9 sounds like the word *canine*, which means "dog."

7

Ruby and her handler won an award for their rescue work.

Ruby finds the boy and licks his face. Her handler follows. Ruby barks so paramedics can find them. Together, they save the boy's life.

SUPER NOSES

Dogs have very strong senses of smell. They can tell one person's smell apart from all others. Some dogs can follow a scent that is many days old.

CHAPTER 2

ON THE JOB

Dogs help the police do many jobs. Dogs often rely on their senses of smell. For example, many K9s do search and rescue. They find missing people.

K9s work in more than 40 countries around the world.

Some K9s are detection dogs. They find missing or dangerous items. Some dogs sniff for drugs. Dogs can also search for bombs or other weapons.

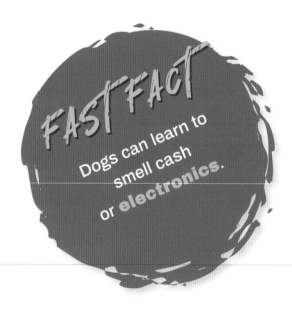

FAST FACT

Dogs can learn to smell cash or electronics.

Detection dogs help the police look for clues or stolen items.

Police dogs learn how to stop suspects from running away.

Dogs may help the police find and catch **suspects**. If suspects run away, K9s can chase them. They can grab and hold suspects until the police catch up.

POLICE DOG BREEDS

Many police dogs are German shepherds. These dogs are large, fast, and strong. However, many breeds of dogs can be K9s. Some detection dogs are quite small.

Detection dogs tend to be breeds with good senses of smell, such as Labrador retrievers.

CHAPTER 3

K9 TRAINING

K9s go through lots of training. Training starts with basic **obedience**. Dogs learn to sit, come, and stay.

Police dog training can take months or years to finish.
Only a few dogs pass.

Next, dogs experience different settings. They enter dark tunnels. They climb metal stairs. They cross slick floors. Dogs jump through windows, too. This prepares them for real-world obstacles.

FAST FACT

Training is like a game for dogs. They earn praise, food, and toys for a job well done.

Dogs also learn specific skills. They practice searching, attacking, and detection. Then they take tests. Dogs that pass the tests become K9s.

During training, dogs get used to many sounds and situations.

Police dogs may be trained to bite and hold a suspect's arm.

BITE TRAINING

Police dogs learn to bite and hold on until called off. Trainers wear padded sleeves or bite suits. Thick fabric keeps the dogs' teeth from piercing their skin.

CHAPTER 4

WORKING AS A TEAM

Each police dog works with one officer. The dog and officer train and work as a team. They can go many places.

Some K9s visit crime scenes. They help look for clues.

K9s often help with **security**. At big events, they help control crowds. At airports, they find dangerous items. They stop people from bringing the items onto planes.

FAST FACT

Some K9s go on patrol with their handlers. They ride in police cars.

A police dog and officer watch a busy street in New York City.

K9s often wear harnesses while they are working. Many have badges, too. Some K9s also wear bulletproof vests. These vests keep the dogs safe.

A bulletproof vest protects the dog's body.

Most police dogs work for about nine years.

A SPECIAL BOND

Police dogs often live with their handlers. They form a close bond. Many handlers adopt their K9s when the dogs retire. They keep the dogs as pets.

COMPREHENSION
QUESTIONS

Write your answers on a separate piece of paper.

1. Write a sentence describing one type of work police dogs do.

2. Would you like to train a police dog? Why or why not?

3. What type of work would a detection dog do?

   A. bite suspects

   B. steal dangerous items

   C. find missing items

4. How does training in different settings help a police dog do its job?

   A. Dogs learn to go many places without being afraid.

   B. Dogs learn not to run very fast or far.

   C. Dogs learn to ignore their handlers.

5. What does **bond** mean in this book?

Police dogs often live with their handlers. They form a close bond.

    A. a faraway place
    B. fear and anger
    C. love or friendship

6. What does **adopt** mean in this book?

Many handlers adopt their K9s when the dogs retire. They keep the dogs as pets.

    A. change shape
    B. own and care for
    C. send away

Answer key on page 32.

GLOSSARY

breeds
Specific types of dogs that have their own looks and abilities.

electronics
Machines that use electricity.

handler
A person who works with and trains an animal.

obedience
Doing what one is told.

obstacles
Things that block the way.

paramedics
People who give emergency medical care.

retire
To stop working a job.

security
The job of keeping something safe.

suspects
People the police think may be guilty of a crime.

BOOKS

Capitano, Madison. *K-9 Units*. Vero Beach, FL: Rourke
  Educational Media, 2020.

Higgins, M. G. *Working Dogs*. Newport Beach, CA:
  Saddleback Educational Publishing, 2020.

Laughlin, Kara L. *Police Dogs*. New York: AV2 by Weigl,
  2019.

ONLINE RESOURCES

Visit www.apexeditions.com to find links and resources
related to this title.

ABOUT THE AUTHOR

Cynthia Argentine likes to discover cool stories and fun facts
for kids. Her books and articles discuss everything from
nature to cybercrime to NASA. She doesn't have a police
dog, but her little white pup keeps her company while she
writes.

INDEX

ANSWER KEY:
1. Answers will vary; 2. Answers will vary; 3. C; 4. A; 5. C; 6. B